Hi Kids,

Join me on an ABC's of Golf adventure with Marvin The Golf Caddy Dog.
Give me a **"WOOF WOOF"** for Marvin!

Text & Illustrations Copyright © 2015 Harold R. Mann. All rights reserved. No part of this book may be reproduced in any form or by any means, including Photocopying, electronic, mechanical, recording, or by any information storage and retrieval system, without permission in writing from the copyright owner. All inquiries should be addressed to: Mann USA, Inc., harold@thebookmann.com

Illustrations by Bob Allen

Published by Mann USA, Inc.
        Omaha, NE 68144
        www.thebookmann.com

ISBN: 978-0-9797322-1-8

Library of Congress Cataloging Number: 2015900107

Printed in the United States of America

10 9 8 7 6 5 4 3 2 1

ABC's of Golf

Harold R. Mann
Illustrated by Bob Allen

Mann USA, Inc.

Happy Golfing,
Marvin

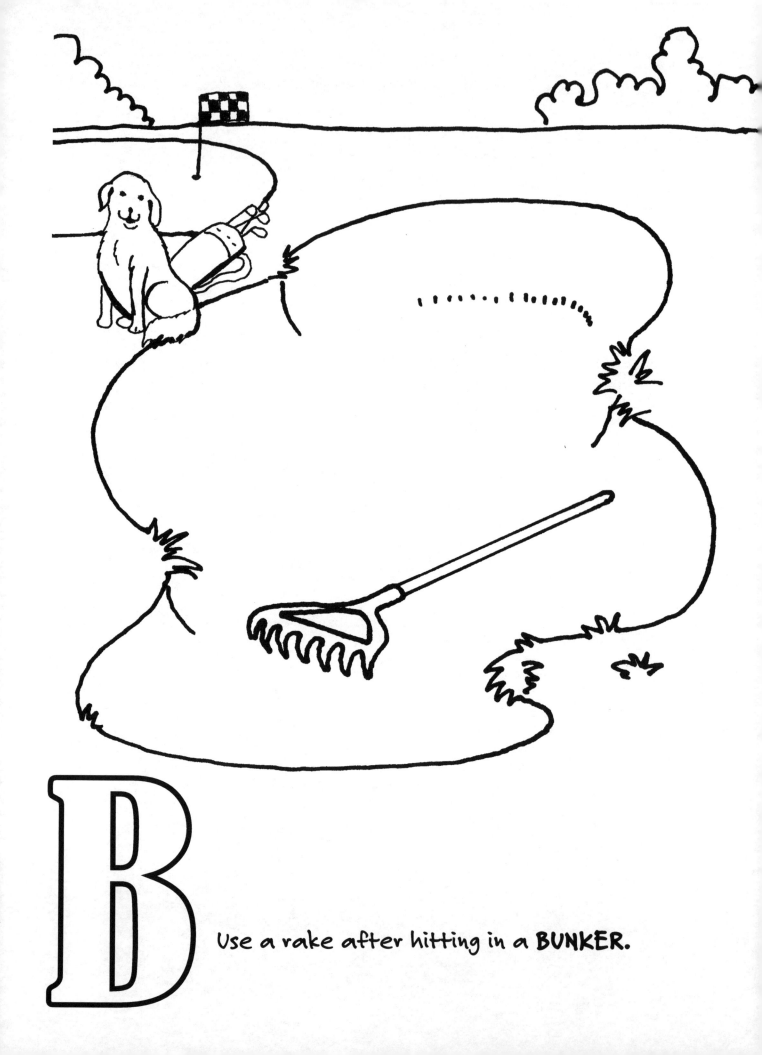

Use a rake after hitting in a **BUNKER**.

Practice your game on the **DRIVING RANGE**.

KNOCKDOWN SHOTS are used to hit a ball low.

K

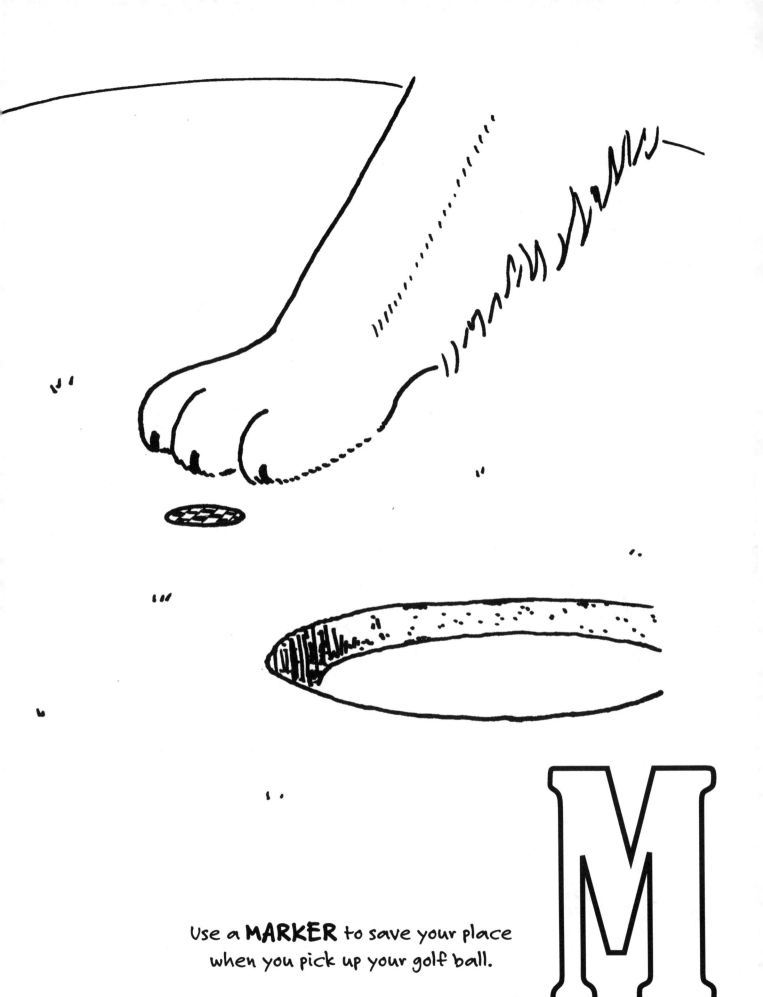

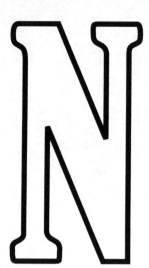

Your score is the total of the **NUMBERS** you write on a scorecard.

Always wear **SUNSCREEN** and a hat when playing and practicing.

T

Use a **TEE** when swinging your driver.

A **WHIFF** is when you swing without hitting the ball.

W

OOPS

An X on a scorecard means no score.

Your distance from the hole is measured in **YARDS**.

Z

Make sure your golf bag **ZIPPERS** are always closed.

MARVIN'S ABC'S LIST OF TERMS

ACE	ACE means a hole-in-one on a Par 3.
BUNKER	Use a rake after hitting in a BUNKER.
CADDY	Marvin is a golf CADDY.
DRIVING RANGE	Practice your game on the DRIVING RANGE.
EXPLOSION SHOT	Always follow through when hitting an EXPLOSION SHOT.
FLAG	Be sure to replace the FLAG after putting.
GLOVE	Wear a GLOVE to hit, but take off to putt.
HEADCOVER	Use a HEADCOVER to protect your golf clubs.
IRONS	IRONS are clubs for shorter distances.
JUNIOR GOLFER	Ted is a JUNIOR GOLFER.
KNOCKDOWN SHOTS	KNOCKDOWN SHOTS are used to hit a ball low.
LOB	LOB shots are used to hit a ball high.
MARKER	Use a MARKER to save your place when you pick up your golf ball.
NUMBERS	Your score is the total of the NUMBERS you write on a scorecard.
OUT OF BOUNDS	White lines, stakes, or fences will show you when you are OUT OF BOUNDS.
PUTTER	The most important club in your bag is a PUTTER.
Q-SCHOOL	Ted dreams of passing Q-SCHOOL to play on the professional tour. (Qualifying School)
ROUGH	The long grass on a golf course is called the ROUGH.
SUNSCREEN	Always wear SUNSCREEN and a hat when playing and practicing.
TEE	Use a TEE when swinging your driver.
UMBRELLA	Don't forget your UMBRELLA on rainy days.
VICTORY	Lots of practice can lead to a VICTORY.
WHIFF	A WHIFF is when you swing without hitting the ball.
X	An X on a scorecard means no score.
YARDS	Your distance from the hole is measured in YARDS.
ZIPPERS	Make sure your golf bag ZIPPERS are always closed.

Marvin
The Golf Caddy Dog

NEW

NEW - Marvin the Golf Caddy Dog
ABC's of Golf Coloring Book

Youth ball cap -
100% cotton twill - Khaki

Golf Towel -
16" x 25"
72% Cotton
28% Polyester

Youth ball cap -
100% cotton twill - Pink

Book 2 - Marvin the Golf Caddy Dog
Qualifies for Junior Nationals

Marvin Driver Cover

Youth Polo -
50/50 poly/cotton
Sizes: S M L XL
Colors: Red, Pink

Book 1 - Marvin the Golf Caddy Dog

TheBookMann.com

Made in the USA
Middletown, DE
23 June 2015